NOW YOU CAN READ A

PETS

TEXT BY STEPHEN ATTMORE

ILLUSTRATED BY

TIM HAYWARD AND ERIC ROWE

BRIMAX BOOKS • NEWMARKET • ENGLAND

Here is a pet store. There are
lots of young animals. No one has
given them names. Can you think
of a name for each one? All the
pets in this shop are for sale.
Would you like one?

Look at the fluffy rabbits.
They are cuddly. Look at the
puppies. They look friendly.
There are so many pets. It is hard
to choose one you like best.
The goldfish is looking at you.

Mary wants a baby
rabbit as a pet.
It is a little
ball of fluff.
It sits in Mary's
hands. Mary calls
it Fluffy.

But Fluffy will
grow—and GROW
—and GROW.
Then it will be
a very big ball
of fluff.

Tom is in the pet
store. He sees
a baby goldfish in
a big tank. It is
pretty. He buys
the baby goldfish
to take home.

He calls his new
pet Goldie. Tom
carries Goldie
home. He is very
careful. He must
not spill Goldie.

All pets need to be looked after.
Some pets like you to cuddle and
stroke them. Mary is picking up
Fluffy. She has one hand on the
neck to steady the rabbit. Look at
the furry pet in the box. This is
a guinea pig. The kitten is
playing a game. It is fun.

Some pets must not be cuddled.
They are afraid. Look at the little
bird in the cage. It is a canary.
The boy must be careful. The canary
might fly away. Tom uses a net
to pick up his pet goldfish.
Goldie must not be out of water
for long or he will die.

Tom is taking Goldie to its new home. His father has made a pond behind the house for goldfish. Now Tom can buy more goldfish. Goldie will have some friends in the pond.

Fluffy lives in a rabbit hutch.
It has two rooms. One room has
wire mesh over the front. Fluffy
likes to look out of her hutch.
She sleeps in the other room
where it is warmer.

What is Fluffy eating? You must give your pet the right food. Ask the people at the pet store. They will tell you what food to give your pet.

This puppy is eating meat. The kitten is lapping milk. You must give your pet fresh food and water every day.

Look at the mice in their cage. They have their food in a little dish. The bottle is full of water. The mice suck water through the tube at the bottom.

Tom is putting fish food on the pond for Goldie. Look at the ring. This stops the food spreading.

Mary is cleaning out the hutch.
She is taking out all the straw.
Then she will put in fresh straw.
Fluffy is in a pen. She is
running and hopping. Mary's friend
Anna is brushing her guinea pig.
This guinea pig has long hair.
Anna brushes it every day.

This is a hamster. Its cage
is cleaned out every few days.
If it is not cleaned out, there
is a nasty smell. Look at
the hamster. It is holding food
in its paws. The hamster stores
some food in its cheeks. That is
why its face looks fat.

It is cruel to keep a pet in
a cage for a long time. Pets
need to run around. Look at the
hamster and guinea pig. They are
in a play pen. It is indoors.

Look at the mouse running inside the wheel. The other mouse is running up the plank.

This tortoise is sleeping. It sleeps all through the winter. It wakes up when the weather gets warmer.

Fluffy has a log in her cage.
She bites the bark with her big
front teeth. This stops the teeth
from growing too long. If they
do grow too long, Fluffy will not
be able to eat.

Many pets have claws. Their claws
may grow too long. Look at the vet
cutting the hamster's claws. A vet
will help you look after your pet.

Here are some other animals.
Would you like one of these
for a pet?

Look for the
insect on the
plant. Can you
find it? It is
a stick insect.

This is a frog.
He lives in the
pond. Tom likes
to watch the
tadpoles change
into frogs.

This is a talking
bird. It is
a parrot.

This is a small
monkey. It is
eating the leaves
in the tree. Can
you think of
a name for this
pet monkey?

This is a goat.
Look at his beard
and his horns.

In this book you have met Goldie
the goldfish and Fluffy the
rabbit. You have also seen other
pets. Look out for these pets.

Goldfish   Dog   Cat   Pony

English rabbit   Rex rabbit   Dutch rabbit